THE LIGHTHOUSE TATTOO

THE LIGHTHOUSE TATTOO

POEMS

JOSE HERNANDEZ DIAZ

ACRE

CINCINNATI 2026

Acre Books is made possible by the support of the Robert and Adele Schiff Foundation and the Department of English at the University of Cincinnati.

Printed in the United States of America

ISBN-13 (pbk) 978-1-968209-08-7
ISBN-13 (ebook) 978-1-968209-09-4

Designed by Barbara Neely
Cover art by Valeria Bojorquez

The press is based at the University of Cincinnati, Department of English, Arts & Sciences Hall, Room 248, PO Box 210069, Cincinnati, OH, 45221-0069.

Acre Books titles may be purchased at a discount for educational use. For information please email business@acre-books.com.

To my parents, Esteban and Maria Hernández.

To my high school English teachers.

To the poetry community.

CONTENTS

III

IV

I

THERE IS A BORDER INSIDE MY AUTUMNAL MIND

Many times, when I meet white intellectuals online or in person,
They want to speak Spanish to me or take a shot of tequila.

No, I'm not ashamed of Spanish, no soy menso, however,
I wouldn't say I grew up speaking Spanish first to strangers.

Assimilation? Perhaps. But as a child one doesn't think so far.
One is just trying to survive, fit in, make friends, enjoy life.

It's complicated, this dual reality, ni de aquí, ni de allá,
But at the same time, very American, very Mexican.

Am I doomed to ambivalence and Mestizaje? I will embrace
This life, strive for clarity amid the chaos clashing in mi vida.

When I visit México, my Spanish improves. I get closer to mi gente.
Walking in the mercado, catching a game of fútbol at the estadio,

Having hamburgúesas on the street, pan dulce in the morning.
But when the plane lands at LAX, I always know I'm home.

Two beautiful homes for one hombre. Why am I complaining?

NI DE AQUÍ, NI DE ALLÁ: NI DE LA PINCHE LUNA

If we call ourselves Mexican American, we are sellouts.
If we call ourselves Chicanos, we are radicals.

If we write in Spanish, we are foreigners.
If we write in English, we are assimilating.
If we write in Spanglish, we have no class.

If we put accent marks on our names, we are trying to prove a point.
If we do not put accent marks, we have once again assimilated.

If we dress like a cholo, we are a threat.
If we dress preppy or like a surfer, we are whitewashed.

If we study Ethnic Studies, we are being difficult.
If we study English Literature, we are Tío Tomas.

If we stick to politics, we are pigeonholed.
If we write about the sunset, we are hopeless romantics.
If we write about the future, we are delusional.

Best to accept these contradictions.
Best to remember our roots.

BIG WAVE SURFING, WOMEN'S BASKETBALL, POZOLE, AND COVID-19

I've avoided Covid for two years but now it has finally hit me.
I'm in my room, alone, fever is climbing. I take Tylenol and it helps

For a while, but I still feel lousy. I lie around in bed, coughing
And nose dripping. I watch a documentary on big wave surfing.

The romance of the eccentric surfer chasing monstrous waves
Reminds me of the allure of poetry and I forget I'm sick for a while.

Also, I watch a documentary about the women's national basketball team from '96.
How one player who grew up rough just wanted to feel appreciated and seen

By her teammates, coaches, and fans, and that is what pushed her.
It reminds me of me and poetry, and what pushes me is respect

In a world that shows little regard, monetary or otherwise, for art.
On the third day of Covid, my mom leaves pozole at my door.

I gulp it up like a monk or prisoner and feel almost cured. No longer
Will I doubt the power of this Aztec medicine. I eat it again

On the fourth day. By the fifth day, I feel better but am still testing positive.
On the sixth day, I finally test negative. I shower, clean my room,

And feel grateful for another day. Another chance to reach my dreams.

MY FATHER TELLS ME HE IS GETTING OLD

His thyroid is acting up; dry. He has high blood pressure.
His prostate is suspicious. His knees are bad.
I can't picture my life without him. I'm a bit of a daddy's boy,

Or man—codependent. I want to name my first-born son
After him, but I'm not a huge fan of the name "Esteban."
Maybe as a middle name? Maybe I won't have a child.

My dad came to this country at a young age.
He sacrificed everything for his family. Getting up at 4 a.m.
To go to work in kitchens and later in waste management.

He wasn't perfect, no, but neither are endings.
Or weather. Or politics. Or memory. My father will always
Be a sacred name in my family, for as long as I live.

I've written poems about him, and that will continue all my life.
I think of James Tate's dad, how he never came back from the war,
On his plane, during Tate's childhood. *Maybe that's why*

He wrote tragic poems? I feel like I understand his poems
More than anyone. No, my father never disappeared,
And he didn't go to war, but I feel like he was only halfway here,

Halfway already gone.

THE NICK VAN EXEL JERSEY

As a kid, I wanted to be Nick Van Exel: "Nick the Quick."
He was the starting point guard for the Lakers when I was growing up.

He was relatively short, quick, and could pass and shoot.
Plus, he was tough. He didn't take anything from anyone.

Nick was a lefty, smooth and quiet, until you crossed the line;
Then he came alive. I could never afford a Van Exel jersey as a kid

Because we grew up low-income, like Nick. However,
I watched every road game, because back then road games

Were on free television. I remember when they traded you, Van Exel.
Not going to lie, it was probably the right move for the team chemistry,

But at the time all I could think about were all those threes
And behind-the-back passes, hyping the crowd up. Nick was gone,

And I never got that jersey, but I'm not looking for pity:
People who grow up in the struggle, when they make it, like Van Exel,

It's that much sweeter, purer. I know I have an arena waiting for me.

HUEVOS REVUELTOS CON CHORIZO

A meal I make often yet don't think about too much.
When I sit and analyze it, though: I realize, I'm in the Southwest.
Do they eat this on the East Coast? Doubt it. They probably

Stick to bagels or pancakes. But I'm on the West Coast.
Formerly, México. Formerly, and still predominanty: indigenous.
I know I'm just having breakfast. Why so serious? It's more than that,

If I investigate the past and see my abuelos and abuelas
Cooking huevos revueltos con chorizo for my tíos and tías. It's a way to carry on
With tradition. I will share this meal with my children one day.

Tortillas, huevos, chorizo, and if you have the patience
To boil the potatoes beforehand: You can add that too!
One difference from my abuelos' time: Nowadays,

You can even replace the pork for soyrizo. ¡Buen provecho!

DEAR WHITE PERSON WHO THINKS I CHARGE TOO MUCH

Do Brown folks deserve professional rates?
What about the minimum professional rate?

Even if we have a fellowship from the National Endowment for the Arts?
What about then, white person, do we deserve a professional rate?

What about, at least, the minimum professional rate, white person?
What if we have years of experience doing the same job

As white people, but better? What about then, white person?
What if we have been published in the best journals

In the world, repeatedly, repeatedly, white person?
What about then? Do we deserve professional rates?

What about the minimum professional rate?
Dear white person? Dear glorious white person?

DEAR WHITE PERSON WHO SAYS I HAVEN'T EXPERIENCED RACISM

Who is the expert on the subject, dear white person?
You, who are looking at it from the outside?

From behind your picket fence with your flag waving?
Or me, the person who has been experiencing

Racism, yes, racism, since birth? So, dear white person,
Who would seem to be the expert on the subject?

You, from a safe and cozy distance, or me, in the trenches,
With the locked doors in the parking lot as I walk by,

The fear in your eyes, as I walk behind you,
In a dark parking lot, with a dark face and dark hands,

Behind you. The dog whistles, the clutched purses,
The utter fear, the fear, and the hate, the hate in your eyes.

FIRST THOUGHTS AS A FIRST-GEN MEXICAN AMERICAN WINNING A FELLOWSHIP

I want to thank my mother and father for their sacrifice.
Coming to this country, penniless. Without speaking English.
Paying their last pesos to a coyote. Not an animal.

A smuggler. The coyote brought them across the desert,
But I don't ask for details. Not once. I'm thankful, today,
As I've won a much-needed fellowship. My parents, though,

Didn't finish elementary school. They had to work on the cerro,
Right away, and help take care of their many siblings.
Both my parents write in a broken language,

But their hearts and smiles are full of hope and love of God.
I'm not religious, but I can tell true believers when I see them.
Tonight, as I toast the highest achievement of my short career,

I'm speechless. Not that a first-gen, low-income kid made it
From nothing. But that I truly always had all I needed:
Familia y amor.

MY LIFE AS AN AVANT-GARDE PAINTER

I paint mostly on stop signs. The word "Go!"
I'm a menace to the suburbs, I should grow up.

I have a canvas the size of the Capitol Records building.
I drip blue paint on it like wind on a mountain.

When I go to the grocery store, I buy an assortment of colors:
Oranges, blueberries, papayas, mangoes.

The cashier tells me to have a great day. I buy four lottery tickets.
I'm not really waiting to be discovered. I've learned

To appreciate those who are already here.
Autumn leaves, my dog, a sunset: These are a few

Of my favorite things to paint. The greats:
Van Gogh, Picasso, Kahlo: They all sought change.

I remember this every day that I paint.

DOLORES PARK CAFÉ

Strong coffee laptop ritualistic Sunday

        Windowpane turkey sandwich flashing stoplight

Across street taxi graffiti in resistance isosceles

        Fragment existence impulsion is implosion

Is routine absorbed and how who knew the scar

        Tearing black-and-white photographic winter

Dolores Park Café pigeons at our feet

SAD CLOWN

I like to bet on horses. Horses and boxing, mostly.
I smoke too many cigarettes. Mine will be a cold hell.

Cold and indifferent. When not mastering my craft,
I dream of being a professional race-car driver. Or a cellist.

Cellists are underrated. So is cash. I wear bright colors
Because I'm afraid of the dark. No one seems to understand

My plight. What does it all mean? The void? In all seriousness,
I have an MFA in Pottery. A BA in Art Theory.

When it comes down to it, Pangaea is a myth.
Religion our only light. These shoes weren't meant

For walking. Drive safely, good night.

BARCELONA, 1933

Dalí is painting. I say, "Wow, that's a good painting."
However, in my head I'm thinking, "He's odd, no, he's intelligent."

Picasso walks in from the patio. I say, "Picasso, where is Olga?"
He starts swinging. Picasso has a good jab and knocks me back,

Then I tackle him, because I'm Chicano. Dalí gets upset.
He is like a demigod to us, so we stop. We start drinking coffee,

Mocking society but loving society. Then Braque walks in.
We say, "Who the hell are you?"

ANOTHER LIFE

I think I was a professional surfer in another life.
Or a boxer. A pugilist, I should say. A writer is a curse.

I think I was a Jack-in-the-Box jester, popping out of said box.
Maybe I was a wolf howling at the moon, wind, clouds.

Or I was a ghost. Because other lives don't exist.
But what if I was a ballerino in the '60s plotting

Against the government? A rebel ballerino—yes!
No, what if I wasn't anything but a poet and a painter?

What if it rained all summer? Snowed in spring?
How do you end a poem? With words. Precious words.

THE ART OF BULLFIGHTING

This is me letting you go. Float away.

Beyond the misty shoreline. Beyond the fading sunset.

Finally, you have exited the dizzying tunnels in my mind.

No longer will I compare you to an out-of-reach rose.

The petals have died. In spite of my open palms.

In spite of the relative calm. Finally, we are free.

To flee. To return to the masquerade.

Looking for the art in bullfighting.

We are wrist-deep in blood.

ODE TO JAMES TATE

If someone held a gun to my head

        And asked who's my favorite poet?

I'd say, What has this world come to

        Where men are held at gunpoint

        For literary aesthetics? And then I'd say,

There are too many to name, the day too short,

        The beach too vast and free to think about

Anything other than riding a longboard

At sunset, flying a kite in early spring,

        But since you are holding a gun to my head,

I guess I'd have to say, James Tate.

II

AUTUMNAL HEART

I woke up from a deep sleep and discovered it was autumn inside my heart. Not that I have a heart anymore. It ran away with a beautiful stripper. My once-present heart was too sensitive for this world anyway. I'm glad it's gone, turned into red leaves, yellow leaves, brown leaves. My faded heart was like an autumn pumpkin, waiting for someone to carve a face on it. I place what is left of my jack-o'-lantern heart in front of my house for Halloween. It scares the neighbors and mail carriers. Monster, ghoul that it's always been.

THE ANNIVERSARY

The anniversary of my death was last Tuesday. I died in a fiery plane crash. I was not a soldier in a heroic war but an adventurist. I discovered many lands. Most of the lands were imaginary, like a dream. One country I founded was called "The Land of Utter Emptiness." It was full of empty wineglasses and cigarette butts. On Sunday, I went to the doctor to check on my health. He said I was, in fact, already dead. Furthermore, it was the anniversary of my death just last Tuesday.

THE IDEALIST

I was abandoned by the army because I believed in the power of flowers to devour our enemies. They called me crazy, said I was an idealist and a dreamer. They abandoned me in the middle of the jungle, not far from the enemy. I began my trek toward the distant coast. I survived on fresh oxalis and snails. For a second, I played dead to avoid a large leopard. I darted around like a fugitive ballerino. I pirouetted with the breeze of the setting sun. When I finally arrived at the ocean, I knelt to my inner compass and thanked the ancient earth. The next day, I'd build a raft and sail away for freedom.

COYOTE

I was looking at photographs of my childhood and there beside me in every picture was a wild coyote. I don't remember having a wild coyote as a pet as a child. A coyote would have, frankly, killed a child is what puzzles me. But there it was, in every childhood memory. Apparently, the wild coyote and I played on the swings together during recess. We shot hoops together as the sun set on summer days. The coyote even attended my First Communion. The coyote always had my back, it turns out, and here I am denying its existence. At least I'll always have these old Polaroid photographs. See you in the next life, dear coyote.

ABUELITA'S PRAYERS

After my abuelita prayed for me, I was suddenly cured of all susto. I no longer feared small talk at the grocery store. I no longer feared standing in front of an audience and reciting depressing poetry. After my abuelita made the sign of the cross on my forehead, I let go of all irrational fear. I applied for jobs I was barely qualified for. I had the confidence of a mediocre white man. I could win them over in the interview, I thought. My abuelita, the darkest one in the family, the one I resemble the most, from Michoacán. She cured me. I am no longer afraid. Susto, no longer part of my vocabulary. I march along, beneath the sun, ready to conquer: Adelante, siempre adelante.

DREAMS OF CONQUEST

I've been having a recurring dream of Hernán Cortés and Cuauhtémoc fighting it out with swords and macuahuitls and shields. My therapist tells me she thinks I'm trying to make sense of my culture and the world at large, as if life should be fair. Fair enough, I tell her, but I don't care who wins anymore. I've had enough. I'm thirty-seven. I just want the fighting to stop. Why can't they just play chess, I ask her. What about a friendly game of basketball or that famous Aztec pelota game—no wait, someone always dies in that game too. I don't want to be obsessed with death anymore, I tell her. I just want to laugh, paint, and enjoy the California weather. As far as dreams go, I tell her, I'd be fine if I just slept through the night.

FIRST IMPRESSIONS OF HELL

The afterlife is exactly what I feared the most. Being naked in front of a crowd while I'm on fire. At first, I start weeping like a baby. I want my mother. I can barely crawl. I feel I can't endure this hell much longer. Then, as if in the middle of a novel, I begin to have an epiphany: There's nothing to be ashamed of. We all look basically the same. Also, fire, once you get used to it, is essentially the same as water. Pain and pleasure, synonymous. It's just a matter of perspective. I light a cigarette from the hellish flames and take it easy the rest of the afternoon. After all, I no longer have to go to work. Joke's on them.

THE BRITISH PHONE BOOTH

I'm stuck inside one of those old red British phone booths from the past. In fact, the only time I hear about phone booths nowadays is when I'm watching boxing and the announcer says, "It's been one hell of a phone booth fight." Outside of the phone booth is rain and fog. No one notices me inside the phone booth. Maybe I like it, after all? Nevertheless, I pick up the phone to call for help. My mother in California answers on the other end. "Try to smash the glass with your fists," she says. I smash the glass, and London fog bleeds into the booth. I crawl out of the phone booth, like a snake. I transform into a Shakespearean marionette, tights, trunks, facial hair and all. I recite the famous sonnets to the eager crowd that has gathered. I'm visible again. I take a bow.

THE PALM TREE PIÑATA

I'm smacking around a piñata shaped like a palm tree. It is Southern California, midsummer. The palm tree piñata is swinging back and forth beneath the bright summer sun. It is my birthday. I'm thirty-eight years old. I don't always act my age, yet I am wise beyond my years, people say. We are having a party to celebrate, a few of my childhood friends are in attendance and many Mexican cousins. We are drinking a mixture of Mexican beers, trendy hard seltzers, and sangria. Finally, I give the palm tree piñata a final smack and it explodes: Out of the piñata comes falling Loteria game sets and Mexican dulces. I pick up a dulce and start chewing. As the sun sets on the West Coast, we play rancheras, cumbias, hip-hop, and oldies, well into the night. The moon rises with the cigarette smoke.

THE HUMAN TREE

I started growing tree branches out of my head and hair after my girlfriend broke up with me. She said I was a lost soul and a bad seed. I told her I'm talented, just a bit disorganized. That's when branches began to dangle from my forehead. Eventually, lush leaves bloomed from the brown branches. I was turning into a tree, all right. I accepted it. After all, I was indifferent. A lost soul, one could say. What did it matter if I had crossed over to plant life? I was alone. Perhaps a bluebird could live among my branches. So long as a woodpecker doesn't destroy my bark, I'll be fine. I'll survive. I always have.

TRAPPED

I'm trapped inside of a prose poem. I can't get out. The lack of line breaks is too liberating, it's anarchy in here. Everyone is doing as they wish, feet up on the coffee table. I saw a man writing graffiti on the governor's mansion—the bravado. The wind is pleasant here. Pleasant like an itch. I wanted to be a short-story writer growing up; I settled for a puppeteer. I like the music in here, jazz and Spanish guitar. If you ask me, I don't think prose poems should last too long. Eventually, you run out of gas, naturally, like a tattooed biker on the interstate. I'm trapped inside of this prose poem, but I don't want to get out. It's nice and cozy in here. I'm invincible.

NEW KID IN TOWN

I was on the subway when I saw a clown, a pirate, and a mermaid. Since I was new to the city, I tried to act casual. The clown was dressed like a bright rainbow; the pirate had his trusty parrot sidekick, per usual; and the mermaid was majestic like the ocean. The funny thing is, nothing extraordinary happened. The clown got off downtown in a hurry. Next, the pirate exited on Main Street, and the mermaid must have gotten off after me. I tipped my Dodgers hat to her as I exited at the circus. I enjoyed my visit to the circus. I saw a man on a tricycle juggling a samurai sword. I saw a lion mimicking ballet. The move to the city was just what I needed.

THE SANDLOT

I don't remember exactly the first time I saw *The Sandlot*. It wasn't in theaters. We didn't go to theaters often as a family; frugal. We probably rented it from the local dollar-video store. Yes, they actually had video stores back in the early '90s. I remember being in awe of the movie, a summertime classic. It came out when I was roughly the same age as the kids in the movie. It was about my life, I thought. Except the kids in the movie played baseball. My friends and I played basketball. Similar to the movie, though, we didn't play organized ball or Little League like the middle-class white kids did. We played on the local asphalt playgrounds until sunset. Further, I admired the fact that Benny "The Jet" Rodriguez looked like me, he was brown like me. *Did he speak Spanish at home, too?* For once, someone who looked like me was on TV, and they weren't a gang member or criminal. *The Sandlot* crew were all just kids, though, exploring youth. That's what I appreciated the most about the movie. Little did I know the real world comes at you fast. Anyway, anytime I see *The Sandlot* on TV, as I'm skipping through the channels, I can't help but remember those summer Southern California nights of youth, watching *The Sandlot* with my brothers and friends, wishing I was Benny "The Jet." Wishing I was part of their crew.

THE FOX

I'm a fox in the woods, my name is Harry. I'm writing a novel, it's called *The Fox and the Field*. I spend most of my days looking for food. Yes, by food I mean small animals, like rabbits. But there's more to me than primitive instinct. I also enjoy classical piano, ballet, and a day off reading Pierre Reverdy. I admire passion at all levels. Us foxes get a bad reputation. Sly, sneaky, untrustworthy. I think I'm more like a saint. Sure, I kill rabbits. But God made me to kill rabbits, frankly. The rest is just fulfilling my duty, playing my role. A fox is a hero. So are you.

THE SURFER

I work at a zoo. I feed the animals and bathe them once a week. Water is the blood of the earth. On the weekends I surf. Sometimes I go on weekday mornings if I have the energy. I once caught a wave that took me away from it all. Not that I hate work, I love what I do. But catching waves takes you to another realm. A zone of freedom, glory, and waves. My father taught me how to surf. He didn't surf himself, he was a blue-collar worker, but he paid for my lessons. On the bottom of my board, I engraved a poem I wrote in his honor.

SUNDAY WAVES

I was at the beach painting a surfer riding a wave onto a canvas when suddenly the ocean water from the painting splashed onto my toes. The surfer came to life in front of my atheist eyes, only, as it turns out, he was the statue of David by Michelangelo. The statue caught some gnarly waves. He was a natural, of course. The statue glided on the water, like a dream. The statue of David showboated for the Lady Madonna statues in the crowd. Somehow, this all made sense to all of us, despite logic. It was Sunday morning, after all. I watched in amazement with the crowd of local surfers and beach enthusiasts. At the end of the session, we gave the statue a standing ovation and said a Hail Mary. "Hail Mary, full of grace. Blessed are the waves."

III

THE LIGHTHOUSE TATTOO

I drifted into the ocean after I got lost in a sailing competition. I drifted far into the middle of the sea. I lost track of time and distance. The waves sounded like a funeral song. I began to feel myself deteriorating. I wrote a farewell letter to my family and friends, but I knew it would likely get buried at sea. I wished I were a dolphin or a seagull; anything that could escape my tortured fate.

Then, a bright lighthouse appeared in the distance, shining through the fog. I was saved. Land was near and hope remained possible, again. As I approached the shore, I jumped off the boat and swam the rest of the way. When I finally made it to shore, I lay on the warm sand and contemplated my luck. I decided when I got back to the city, I would get a lighthouse tattoo on my shoulder. It was a traumatic ordeal; the only thing I knew was life is fickle, like a feather in the wind.

GARCÍA MÁRQUEZ, THE ROOSTER

My dog barks at the poor mail carrier and I see fear in both their eyes. I yell at the dog to relax and act civilized. The sun goes down at 6 p.m. and I have a few hours before bed, then work, then the whole routine again.

The next day my rooster, García Márquez, doesn't wake us up. I go outside to check on him. He's dead. Murdered by the CIA, I'm assuming. I call the cops, but they tell me the CIA is a fine organization. I bury my rooster, García Márquez, with my medals from football and wrestling. García Márquez was a fine rooster, I tell the crowd who's gathered, mostly local bikers and misfits. García Márquez would sing to the sun every morning, as if it were a newborn. Now, he is in heaven, with Jesus, Mary, and the lambs. *We'll see you soon, old friend.*

ALBERT CAMUS, THE ALIEN

It is fall. My favorite season. I go outside to take out the trash and instead of dead leaves on the ground, I discover a spaceship. An alien climbs out of said spaceship. They wear a shiny silver suit with a logo of the planet Jupiter on the breast pocket. The alien speaks in perfect French. In fact, their name tag reveals they are named Albert Camus, I'm assuming after the writer. The alien is red and yellow, like a McDonald's sign. They are neither aggressive nor passive. They are moderate in their manners. As the alien approaches me, they begin to sing an ancient alien song. They are rather proud when they sing. I shut the door on the alien and immediately call the cops. The alien begins to weep, and I instantly regret calling the cops. Startled, the alien returns to the spaceship and flees home. I tell my friends this story every autumn when the leaves begin to fall, and they insist I'm crazy. Granted, I'm a little out there, but the alien certainly crashed in my backyard that evening, like a pile of dead leaves.

THE LEGEND OF THE FALL

I fell from a giant polka-dot hot-air balloon up in the sky. Just as I fell from the balloon, it began to rain English breakfast tea. What cushioned my fall was a pile of hand-me-down clothes from my youth. They were too big for me because my older brother is a few inches taller than I am. My mother was in the garden cutting nopales for breakfast. I ran into my mother's adobe home from childhood because I missed summertime in México. Once, when I was thirteen, my friends and I played soccer for twenty-six consecutive days, on the cerro, without sleep. At one point, we were playing in front of the International Guinness Book of World Records officials. We didn't end up breaking the record, though. We fell just short. Short of immortality and legend. The legend of the fall.

MY BATTLE WITH AN ENGLISH DRAGON

I lay down to sleep after a long day painting apartment buildings for $25 an hour. That's when I started dreaming about a medieval dragon. It was an English dragon, no doubt, from childhood years of too many fairy tales. I was dressed in the skin of a jaguar I had hunted. I wasn't an Englishman. I was a Mexican from Southern California. I chased the dragon on my motorcycle. I chased it along the Pacific Coast Highway. The dragon was trying to destroy the West Coast. In the dream, I was a Jaguar knight mixed with a conquistador, but I was fighting a scarlet dragon. The dragon looked like it belonged in an English folk tale or an epic poem written by a hermit. Anyway, I battled the dragon with my macuahuitl, but since I'm mestizo, I also had a sword and shield. I slew the dragon with a swift strike to the heart. It fell on the sand and was eventually pulled into the sea. I rode my motorcycle home as the moonlight sparkled on the ocean.

MEETING CAL RIPKEN JR. FOR COFFEE ONE MORNING

I was having my morning cup of coffee; the sun was getting ready to attack the Southern California area. It was midsummer. Then, someone knocked on my front door. It was Cal Ripken Jr. I almost started crying I was so surprised. I asked Cal to autograph my Los Angeles Dodgers coffee mug. He laughed and signed it. I thanked him for breaking the consecutive games record against the Angels and told him it inspired me as a child. I asked why he was here. "Because you're my favorite author," he said. "But I haven't published anything but obscure prose poetry," I told him. "That's what I'm into," he said. "What a small world," I said. I signed a couple priceless (literally priceless) literary journals for Cal, and he was on his way, happy as an Oriole.

THE FORTUNE TELLER OF MY YOUTH

after Mary Ruefle

When I was young, a fortune teller told me I'd slay many dragons with nothing but a silver rose. The fortune teller told me I'd bring great pride to my family, building a baroque castle for all of us to reside in. The fortune teller, whom I met in a peaceful dream, said I'd fly amongst giants but retain the heart of a lamb. Sometimes, I think of this fortune teller, at the dawn of autumn, when the leaves begin to turn brown, and the thick fog obscures the midnight moon.

THE IMMORTAL ONES

I was lifting weights at the gym when suddenly I was surrounded by a crew of Jaguar Knights from the fifteenth century. We left the gym right away and headed to the southern jungles. I was told I would eventually have to wrestle a jaguar for my right to live. They all laughed. It was a harmless joke. I immediately trained in the art of weaponry, which resembled a ballet with sharp swords. I hardened the nerves in my legs to feel as little pain as possible. All the exercises and training took place at midnight beneath the jaguar moon. When the war of the flowers eventually came, I charged the enemy without fear. I became immortal.

EL BOXEADOR

I've been a boxer since I was five years old. I grew up on the southeast side of town. No one really wants to live here except us Mexicans. My father always wanted to be a professional fighter, but he mostly just watched it on the weekends, with a beer. He worked as an industrial mechanic for thirty-five years. That's how he paid for my boxing training. When he saw I didn't care much for tools, he taught me the right hook. He said, "We are Mexican fighters. We rarely use the jab. We are undersized but our hearts are made of iron. We get in on the inside, like Canelo fighting those tall light heavyweights. We come from an Aztec warrior class. Boxing isn't a sport, mijo," he'd say, "it's a religion. The boxing Gods don't forgive."

FREE AS A MIME

They say one shouldn't talk about the avant-garde, like *Fight Club*—oh well, no one is around to listen to me. I go about my day rhyming near rhymes, never perfect. I like to hit on prima ballerinas from Russia on Instagram. It makes me feel important when they respond. Once, in church, as a young boy, I got to hold the Candle of the Ascension during Easter service.

Aesthetically, I avoid famous writers, like Mary Oliver or Billy Collins, except I'm secretly a huge Billy Collins fan. Writers say the best way to a word, a line, or a poem is directly. I say the best way to a word, a line, or a poem is directly, but with good editing. What is it, exactly, about a street mime on the boardwalk that comes off as romantic? I wish I were as free as a mime. Wish I had the guts to stand in front of an audience and just dance, without making a sound. If I get discovered one day and reach fame, I hope it will be on my terms. Or at least until I get tenure. Until then, it's whatever the department wants. Ultimately, it's just about dollars and cents, amigo. Buying property with a picket fence. This is America, after all. Land of the capitalist swine.

LIFE OF A POET

I was getting a haircut at the local Supercuts because I'm square and suburban. I feel like a new man every time I get a cut, it's the best. The barber, per usual, was reassuring me about my life and congratulating me on all my success. I felt comfortable, like watching college football in my pajamas on a Saturday morning. No obligations, just smooth sailing. However, I must've jinxed myself with the Aztec Gods with this sense of ease, because after my haircut my debit card was declined. I thought for sure I had enough funds in the account. How could I be so careless? It was so embarrassing. All I spend on is groceries, gas, and bills. No stylish clothes. No going out to bars. I asked the barber what to do. They said to just pay next time. I apologized profusely. I walked out of there like a sad dog with his tail between his legs.

When I got home, though, I saw I got a letter in the mail from Stanford University. I opened it like a Mexican kid on Christmas Eve. I had won a prestigious poetry prize: $3,000. I pumped my fist in the air. "Fuck yes!" I said. Right away, I went and cashed the check and immediately paid the barber for the haircut. "Life of a poet!" I said to the barber, laughing.

ANTONIO AGUILAR, THE ROOSTER

A painter woke to the memory of a rooster's song. However, it was two o'clock in the morning. Nevertheless, he picked up his favorite easel and went downstairs to make a cup of coffee. He made it strong with a bit of sugar. It was the last day of summer. The leaves had begun to fall at sunset, or was it merely always autumn in his heart?

After he ate a breakfast of chorizo con huevos y café, he gathered his painting supplies. He painted a rooster with a traje de charro and a colorful rooster head. Then he painted a simple sun with a smiling face. The rooster's name was Antonio Aguilar. At sunrise, in the painting, the rooster sang famous rancheras to the suburbs of Los Ángeles.

THE BLUE ROOSTER AND THE ORANGE MOON

In the middle of the nineteenth century within the countryside of France, there was a blue rooster who was afraid of the orange moon. The blue rooster slept all night until the orange moon was long gone. It feared the eeriness of the moon. Sometimes, it had nightmares about the orange moon. Then one day, the orange moon appeared extremely early, before sunset. The blue rooster ran around in circles, as if headless. It shrieked a bizarre ancient cry amidst the chaos. Finally, the blue rooster fell to the ground and collapsed. It fell asleep, like a newborn. As the orange moon faded away the next day, the blue rooster slowly arose, like a river. Slowly, like the sunrise.

MEETING PANCHO VILLA AT A PARK ON THE SOUTHEAST SIDE

I was riding my bike at a local park on the southeast side of town. It was a Sunday morning at the end of May. The sun was mild, and spring was almost over. Just as I sat on a bench to take it all in, I saw the ghost of Pancho Villa smoking a cigar on an adjacent bench, with a large brown horse at his side. I went up to him. "Un honor, General," I said. "The pleasure is mine," he said. "You speak English?" I said, shocked. "No, but this isn't necessarily reality," he said. "What do you mean?" I asked. "Have you considered that I've been dead for decades. You are merely imagining me," he said. "Why would I imagine Pancho Villa on a lazy Sunday at the park? I haven't taken any drugs," I said. "You romanticize the past, like many, hiding behind your cultural heroes to avoid simple pleasures, like a casual day at the park," he said. "Fascinating," I said. As I thought about what Villa said, he suddenly disappeared, horse and all, in a puff of cigar smoke. The sun was shining a little stronger at this point. Still, I decided to play a game of pickup basketball with the locals and then went home to rest for the workweek ahead.

"POPULARES" GAMESA COOKIES

When I was growing up, my mom never really mentioned we were poor. She also didn't always mention she grew up poorer, in México. Most of my memories of her revolve around her singing church songs in the kitchen, in both English and Spanish, as she prepared pancakes or bean-and-cheese burritos or quesadillas. Or when she would yell at us, of course, this time always in Spanish, to quit saying bad words or quit being "huevones" and clean up around the house.

Now, a grown man, I'm at my mother's kitchen table and she walks in from the 99-Cent store. She has groceries with her, per usual, but she makes a point of showing me a box of Mexican cookies called "Populares" from the brand Gamesa. She tells me when she was a little girl in México, her siblings would get super excited when my abuelos brought the cookies home for a special snack. She said they would share half a cookie with each sibling so everyone could have a taste. I open the box and examine the cookies. They look like the most basic sugarless cookies that no American child would ever lust for. I tell my mom that it is a "great story" with a straight face, but inside I realize how deep the story really is.

Every time I feel sorry for myself, in fact, I try to think of the Gamesa "Populares" cookies. I think of how Mom always buys a big box now, just because she can afford it. I think of how tasteless those cookies are and how coveted they were to my beloved ancestors. *Cookies*, I ponder, *who would've thought? Who would've thought life could be so unfair?*

LITTLE LEAGUE, AMERICA

Growing up, I always wanted to play Little League baseball or organized basketball, whatever it was called back then. I knew we couldn't afford it, so I didn't make a big deal about it to my parents. Maybe I asked once or twice, but I always knew what the answer was going to be. I did, however, play a lot of street basketball at the local parks with my friends, who also lived in low-rent apartments in middle-class suburbs. My friends and I never really talked about Little League, but I remember one time, on my way to the asphalt courts, I stopped by the lush Little League field at the park and watched the mostly suburban white kids playing baseball with their new uniforms, which mimicked the team names of the big-league clubs. Was I jealous? I don't remember—probably, though. No, I didn't use it as inspiration to achieve. I didn't cry about it at night, either. I just wanted to be out there, with my schoolmates, playing shortstop on a Little League field, in the country I loved.

ONE HUNDRED YEARS OF GRATITUDE

It wasn't easy growing up low-income, first-generation Mexican American in Southern California. Sometimes, it felt like we weren't supposed to speak Spanish in front of "mainstream" Americans. Sometimes, it felt like we had to hide the fact we were poor. Get dropped off in our parents' old beat-up car a block or two away from school, so as not to be seen. No, it wasn't our fault (as if poverty was ever anyone's fault), we were fully employed, just had the cards stacked against us.

But this isn't where I cry or bleed out or get saved. Except by my older sister, Letty, who paved the way. The first in the family to graduate college, or high school for that matter. The first to be an English major. Then, I became an English major. Then, my little sister too. And other siblings chose different majors. We overcame, yes, with the help and sacrifice of our parents. It wasn't easy growing up the way we did. But it definitely united us. Made us stronger. It pushed us, pushed us, pushed until we had to punch our way out. Kick down every bolted door, so the next generation might have it easier.

IV

THE MOON, 2050

A man in an At the Drive-In shirt bought a new car because his old car had disintegrated. The new car was a flying car. It was the year 2050. The man in an At the Drive-In shirt flew in his flying car to the zoo, except the zoo was on the Moon. When the Moon had first been colonized in 2025, the Americans brought baby zebras there to start building the species on the Moon. Eventually, there were too many zebras roaming free. They were rounded up by astronauts and placed in a zoo. The zoo of zebras was a major attraction on the Moon. Right next to the ballet of penguins. When the man in an At the Drive-In shirt finished his day at the zoo of zebras and the ballet of penguins, he had an iced coffee at Earth set. "The Earth is so old-school and nostalgic," he said to himself as he sipped his iced coffee.

THE MAN AND THE DRAGON

> People who deny the existence of dragons are often eaten by dragons. From within.
>
> —URSULA K. LE GUIN

A man in a Jimi Hendrix shirt walked a dragon to a liquor store. The dragon was named Louie the Dragon. The dragon was purple and green. The man in a Jimi Hendrix shirt tied the dragon to a pole outside of the liquor store as he purchased marigolds and an umbrella. It was only slightly raining, a drizzle.

Next, the man in a Jimi Hendrix shirt jumped on the dragon and flew over the freeway in the jagged city. The man saw cars and buildings below; he felt like a star. The dragon only obeyed his owner, the man in a Jimi Hendrix shirt. He had nurtured the dragon since infancy.

The man in a Jimi Hendrix shirt finally arrived at a Gothic cemetery. The man laid flowers on the dragon's mother's grave. He'd promised to take care of her baby dragon until it grew strong and independent. The man in a Jimi Hendrix shirt and the dragon sat by the grave until sunset and then flew back to the suburbs.

AN ODE TO THE CALIFORNIA BURRITO

A man in a Chicano Batman shirt surfed in the ocean. It was late summer. He grew up driving the hour and twenty minutes' distance from Southeast Los Angeles to the coast. Instead of wearing a traditional wet suit, today he wore a Chicano Batman shirt because it was a hot summer day, and the water wasn't too cold. He caught some decent waves and then lay out on the sand to read a book of poetry by the Uruguayan writer Marosa di Giorgio.

After he finished reading, he went to a taqueria across the street. He had a California burrito. The California burrito consists of carne asada, fries, pico de gallo, cheese, and guacamole. He had an horchata alongside the burrito. It was the man in a Chicano Batman shirt's go-to meal when he was looking for comfort food. When he finished the burrito, he drove home. The sun began to set. When he got home, he showered and then wrote a song about his day. He called it "An Ode to the California Burrito."

THE FAIRGROUNDS IN THE RAIN

A man in a Chicano Batman shirt and sunglasses went to the fair in Southeast Los Angeles. It was late summer. He rode the bumper cars. He rode the Ferris wheel. The man in a Chicano Batman shirt bought a hot dog on a stick and a glass of lemonade. He tried to get a large ball into a small hoop but was instead swindled for $5. He laughed it off.

Then it began to rain. Most folks went home. The man in a Chicano Batman shirt decided to wait it out. He sat beneath some palm trees and pulled out a sketchbook. He drew the fairgrounds in the rain. It brought him peace and pleasure to draw. It didn't stop raining, though, so he eventually went home. The next morning, he painted the drawing from the fair onto a canvas. He used rather dark tones for the clouds and the rainfall juxtaposed with bright colors for the rides and concession stands. He titled the piece "The Fairgrounds in the Rain."

GUISADOS

A man in a Chicano Batman shirt drove on the 5 freeway northbound, headed to Los Angeles. He was going to Guisados, a taqueria; they have some of the best tacos in town. The man in a Chicano Batman shirt had just gotten off work as a substitute English teacher in Southeast LA County.

The traffic was moderate at 3 p.m. He arrived in Boyle Heights in thirty minutes. Once inside the restaurant, he ordered four tacos: two salsa roja tacos and two steak picado tacos. He also ordered a Coke. The not-so-secret to the tacos is that they are slowly cooked in stew for rich flavor. While the man in a Chicano Batman shirt ate the tacos, he admired the artwork on the restaurant walls. There was a painting of a bullfighter with a rose between his lips. A painting of various Mexican luchador masks. There were also some artful photographs of everyday life in Boyle Heights. When the man finished eating, he tipped his Dodgers hat and said "Gracias" to the owner and staff. As he drove back home to Norwalk, he kept thinking, the tacos are a bit pricey, but they are definitely the best in town.

LA LIBERTAD

A man in a Chicano Batman shirt goes to a park in Northeast LA to play soccer or fútbol with some friends. He used to play in high school too, but he quit to focus on political science and debate. He recently graduated from USC with a master's in public policy. His goal, no pun intended, is to work for a professional soccer team one day: LAFC.

The man in a Chicano Batman shirt arrives at the park and begins to warm up with his friends. They are all first-gen or second-gen Latinx folks from the neighborhood. When the game starts, the man in a Chicano Batman shirt scores two goals, one with his head and the other from the penalty area. His team celebrates by jumping up and down and chanting in a circle. After the game, they meet up at their local brewery. They have local brews and pizza. The man in a Chicano Batman shirt has an horchata ale. It's called "La Libertad." At the end of the night, the man in a Chicano Batman shirt drives home beneath the moonlight, listening to Gary Clark Jr.

EL TÍO IN A MARS VOLTA SHIRT

A tío in a Mars Volta shirt played tetherball at the park with his niece. He was proud of being an uncle. His niece was dark-skinned Mexican, like him and his abuelita too. The tío in a Mars Volta shirt played tetherball with his niece and then they went to In-N-Out for burgers. When they finished eating, they went to an old record store. The tío in a Mars Volta shirt showed his niece a guitar. She liked it. They bought one.

Within a couple of weeks, his niece was enrolled in guitar lessons. Her favorite band was Pink Floyd, like her tío. It was kind of boring to her, honestly, but she liked that they shared that. The tío in a Mars Volta shirt showed his niece how to play a ranchera on the guitar. They laughed and played until sunset.

HEREDITIES

A man in a Selena Quintanilla shirt walked along the shore. It started to rain. The rain soaked his hat. The man in a Selena Quintanilla shirt took off his hat and threw it into the ocean.

When the man in a Selena Quintanilla shirt was a boy, he'd ride the bus to the beach in the summer with his tío. His tío taught him how to surf and draw. His tío was a surfer and a painter.

Now, the man watched the sunset on the coast of Southern California. His tío eventually became a teacher for his community. The man in a Selena Quintanilla shirt became a muralist and a poet.

ACKNOWLEDGMENTS

Grateful acknowledgment is made to the following literary journals, where some of these poems first appeared, sometimes in different forms:

The Acentos Review
Air/Light
Allium, A Journal of Poetry & Prose
ANMLY
Bennington Review
Blue Earth Review
Booth
Brazos River Review
Chicago Quarterly Review
Dialogist
Fourteen Hills
Hex Literary
The Ilanot Review
Interim
Invisible City
The Laurel Review
Litro Magazine (UK)
The Lumiere Review
The Maine Review
Midway Journal
The Moth Magazine (Ireland)
the museum of americana
The Offing
Olney Magazine
Passengers Journal
Puerto del Sol
Red Ogre Review (UK)
South Florida Poetry Journal
Sugar House Review
Sweet Literary
Water~Stone Review
The Westchester Review
The Worcester Review
Zócalo Public Square